Reflect and Unwind
Mandalas & Designs
Coloring Book for Adults

David Rich Sol

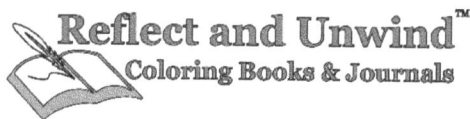

Reflect and Unwind™
Coloring Books & Journals

First Printing, November 2015

Published by: Reflect and Unwind Coloring Books & Journals, an imprint of
Green Tomato Publishing, LLC.

http://www.ReflectandUnwind.com

ISBN: 0692589996
ISBN-13: 978-0692589991

INTRODUCTION

Sit back, relax and unwind through the fun and creative process of coloring in each of the thirty designs included in this book. Within these pages, you will find a mix of both simple and elaborate illustrations created for your enjoyment.

For best results, we recommend you use color pencils as the best media in coloring these designs. However, we have only printed one image per double-sided page, in this way, you can explore the use of other media including markers. As certain markers may bleed through the page, we would recommend you place an extra blank sheet of paper under the image you are coloring with a marker.

Be creative, have fun and discover a positive way to relieve tension and stress.

Consider using colors that complement and look good next to each other. Here is a helpful list of complementary colors for your reference:

Red	complements	Green
Red-Orange	complements	Blue-Green
Orange	complements	Blue
Yellow-Orange	complements	Blue-Purple
Yellow	complements	Purple
Yellow-Green	complements	Red-Purple

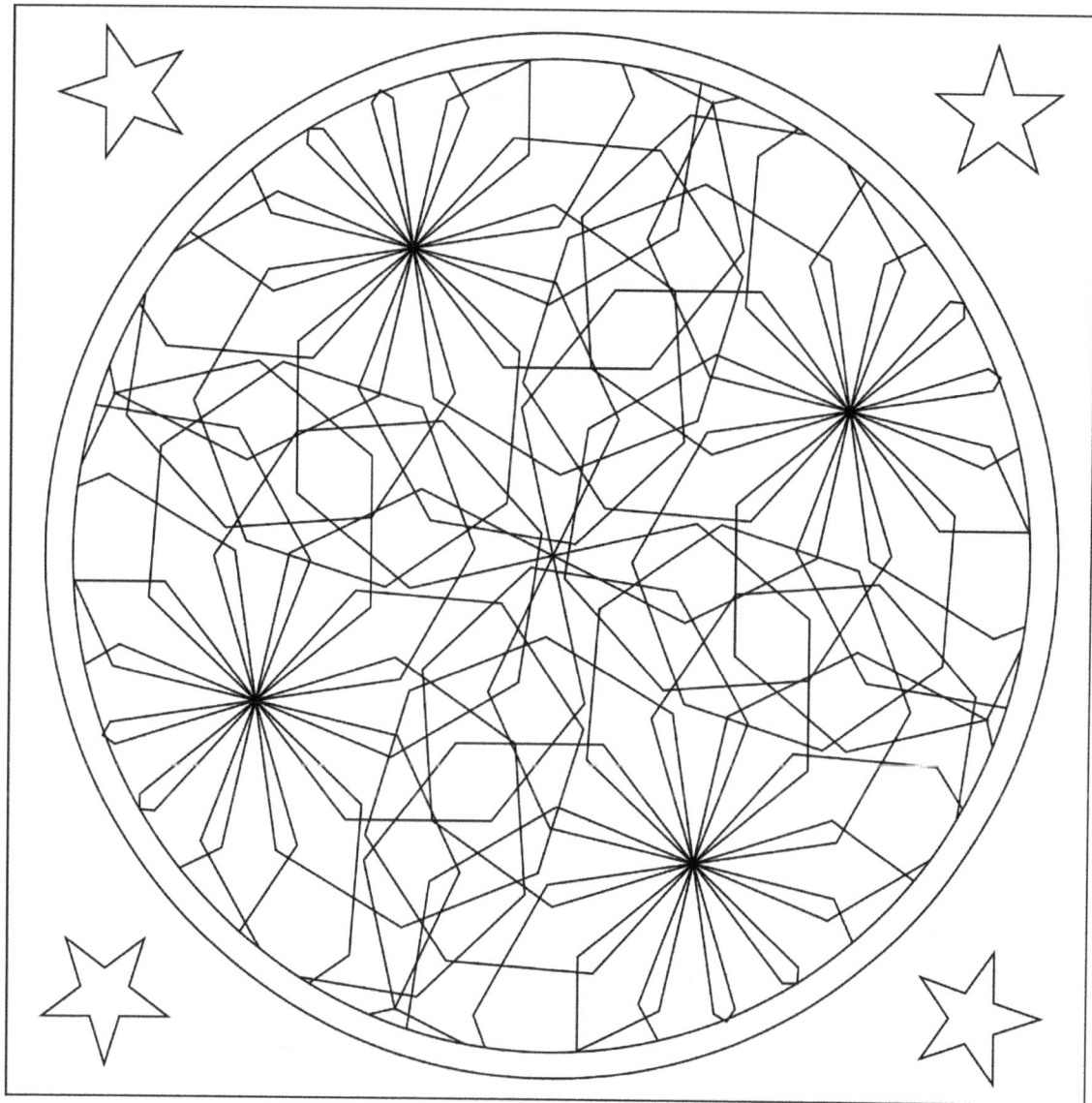

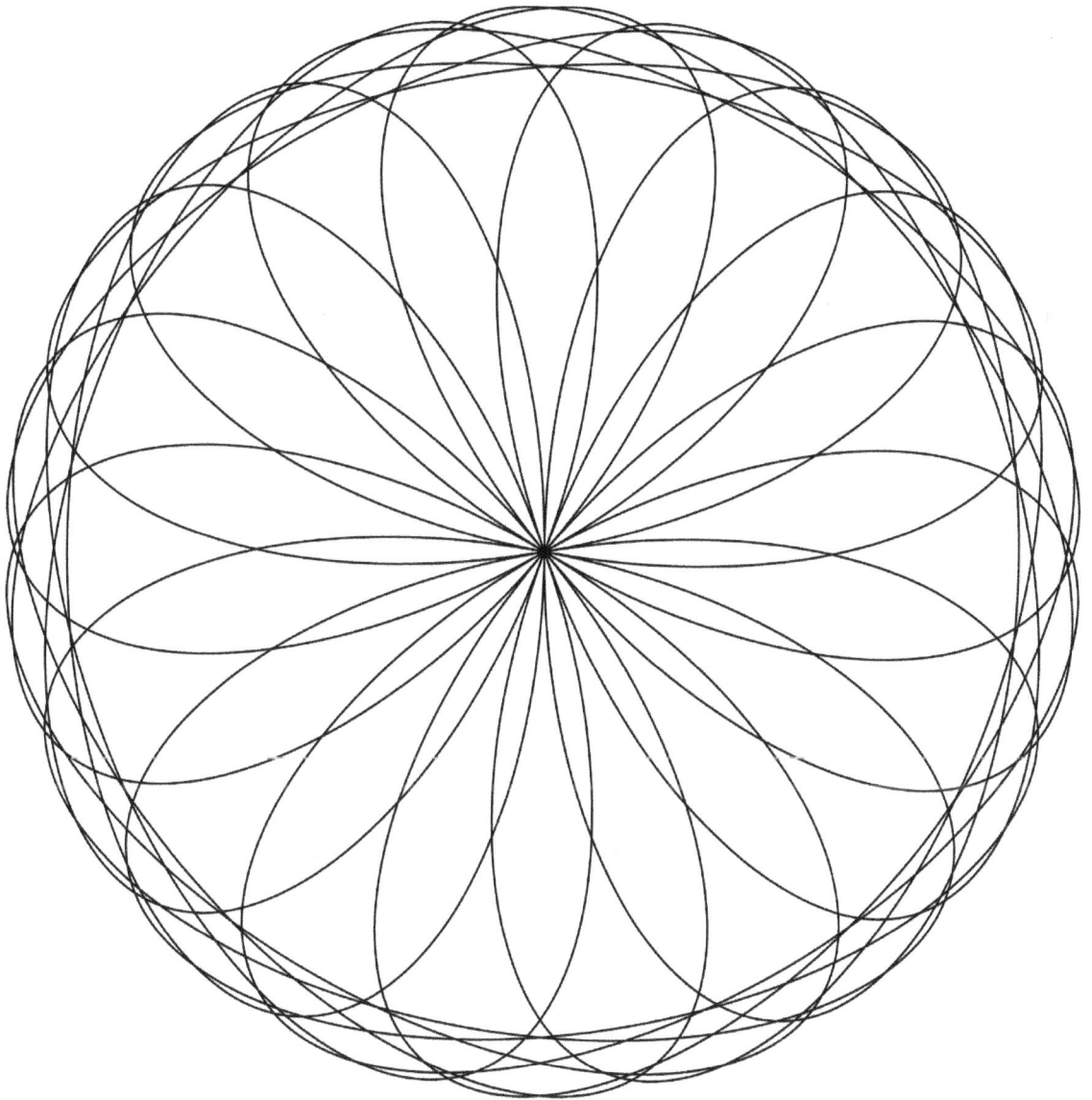

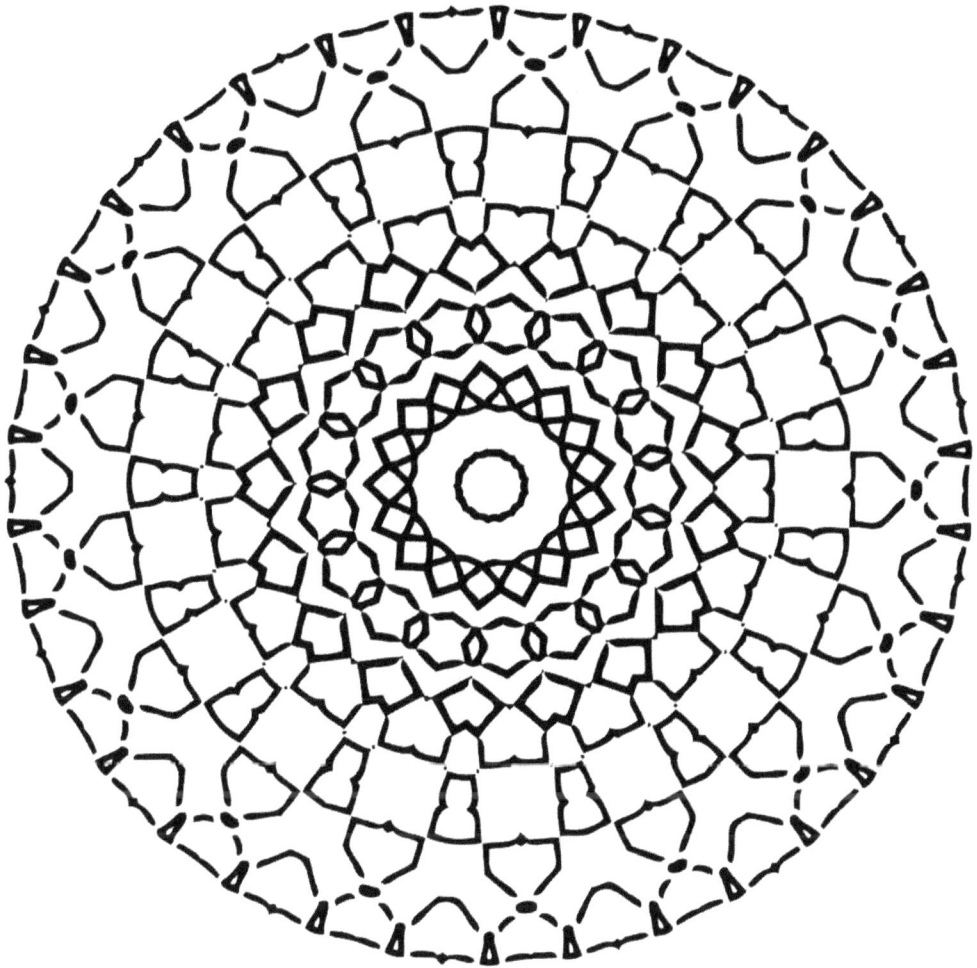

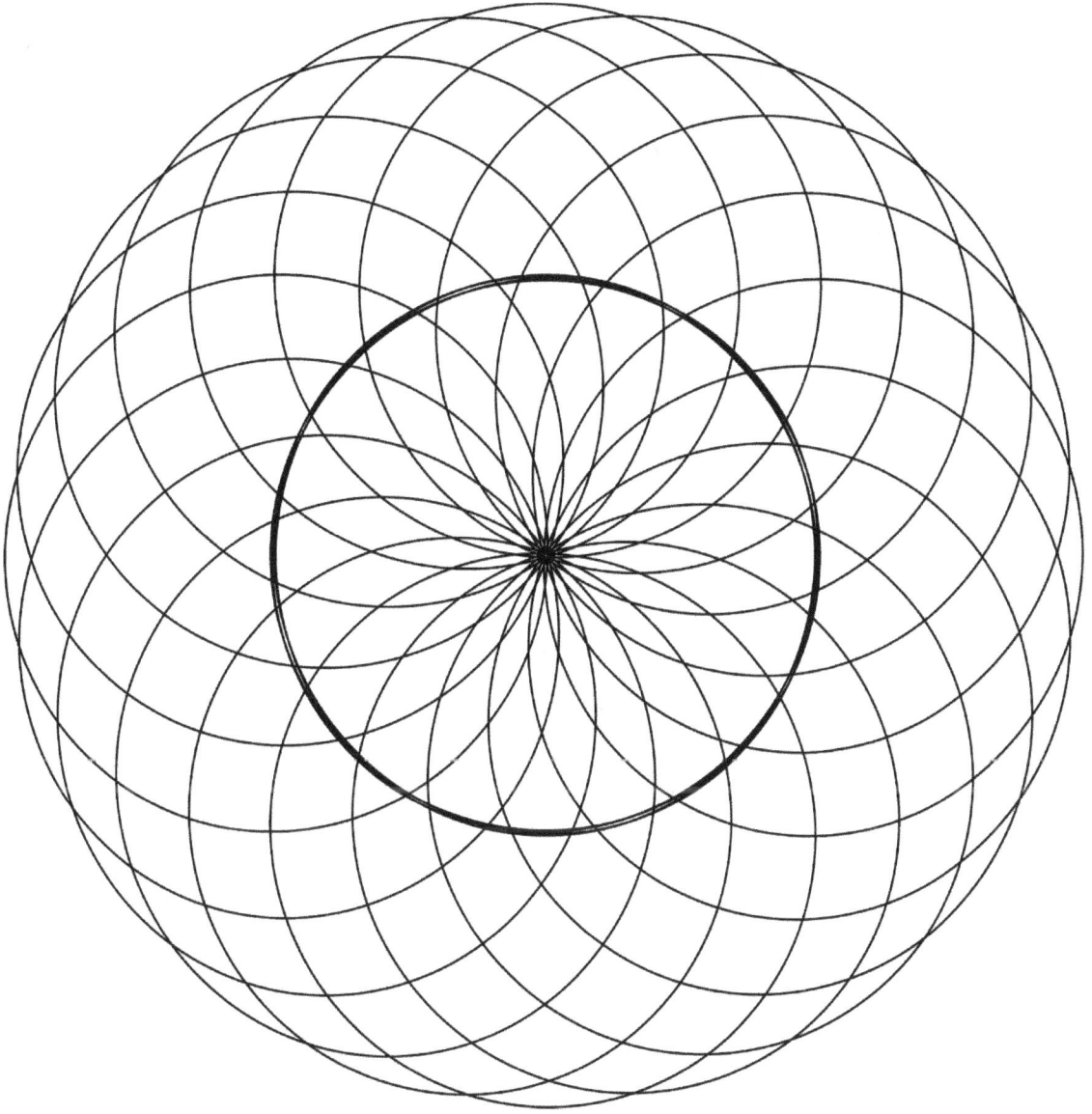

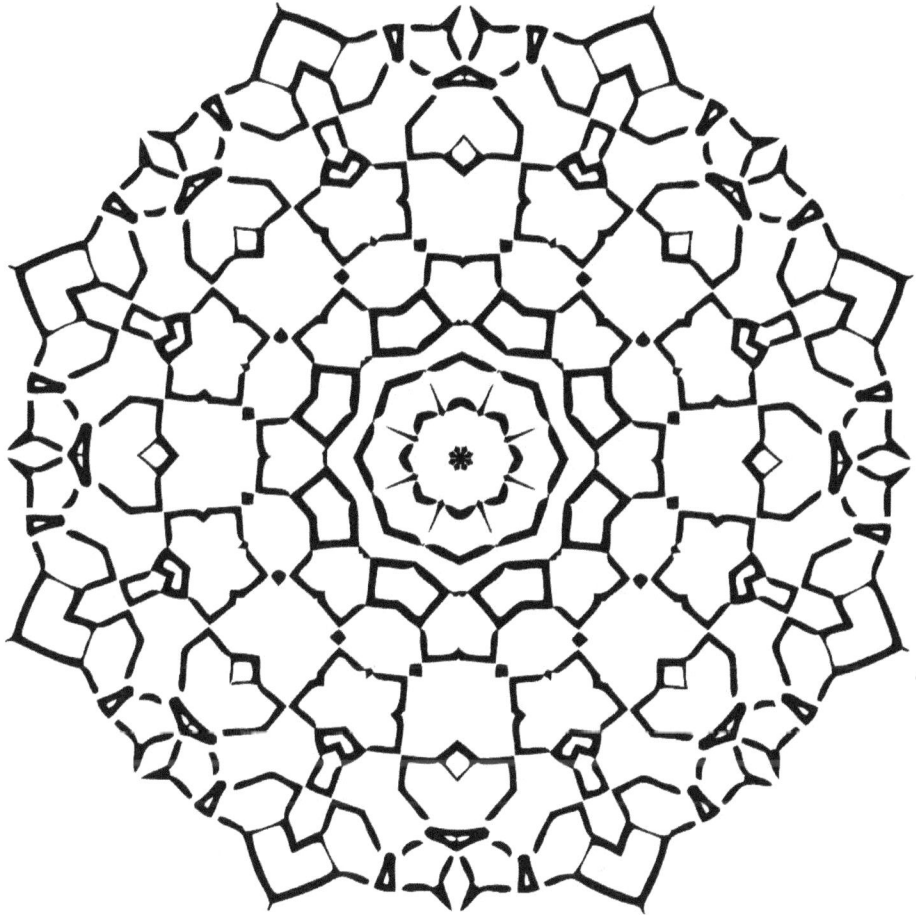

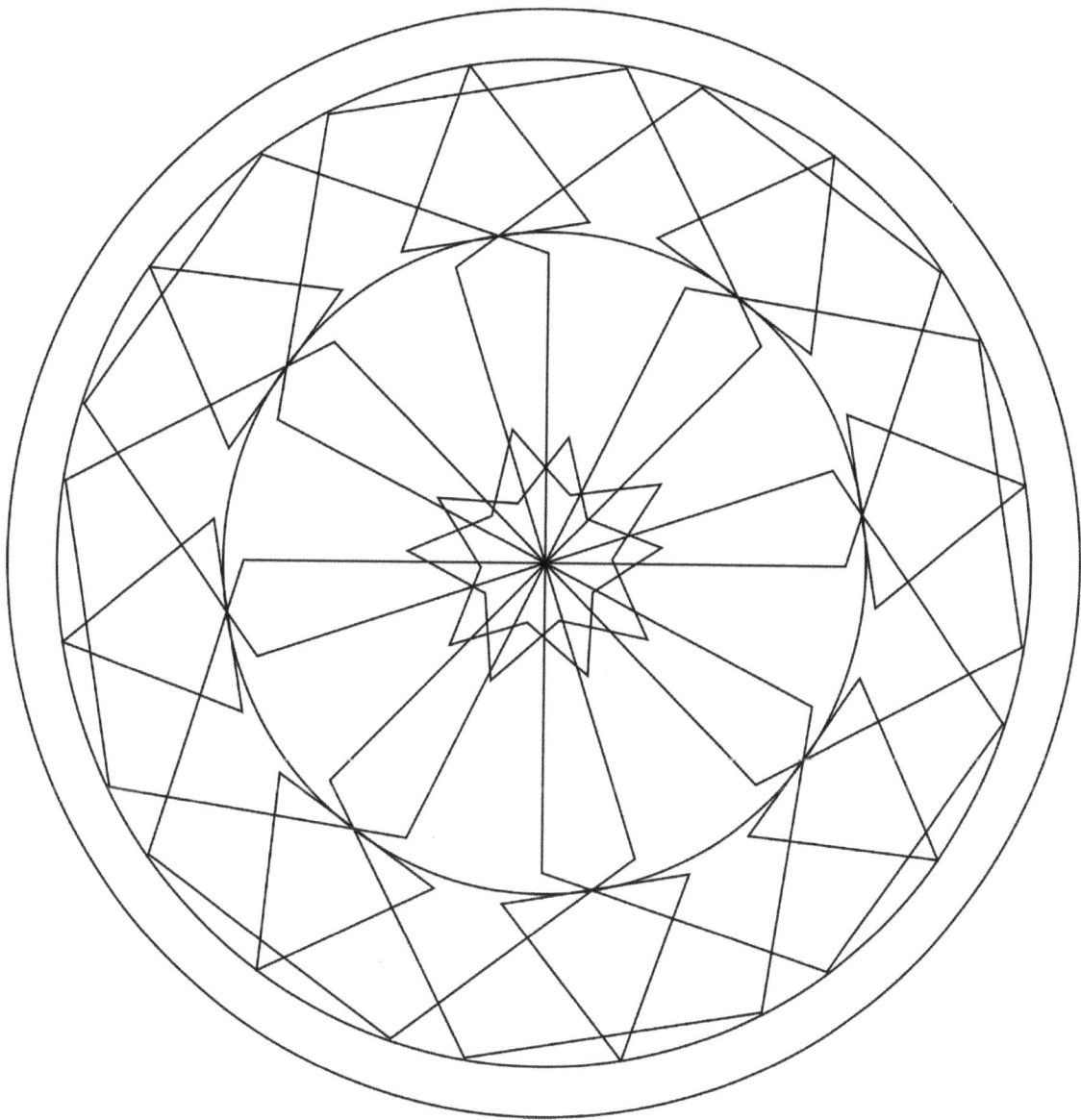

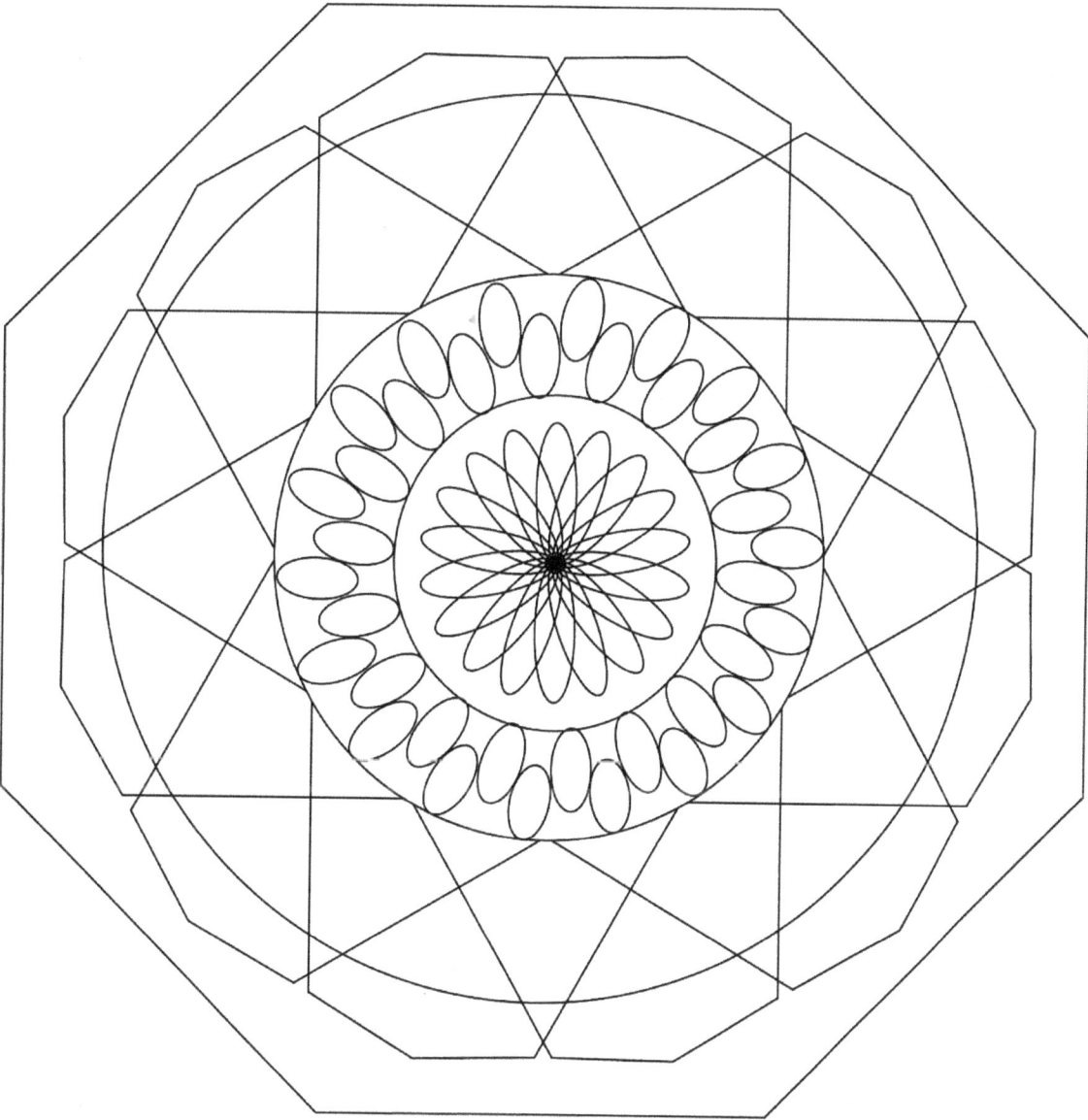

RELAX, REFLECT AND UNWIND WITH OUR OTHER BOOKS:

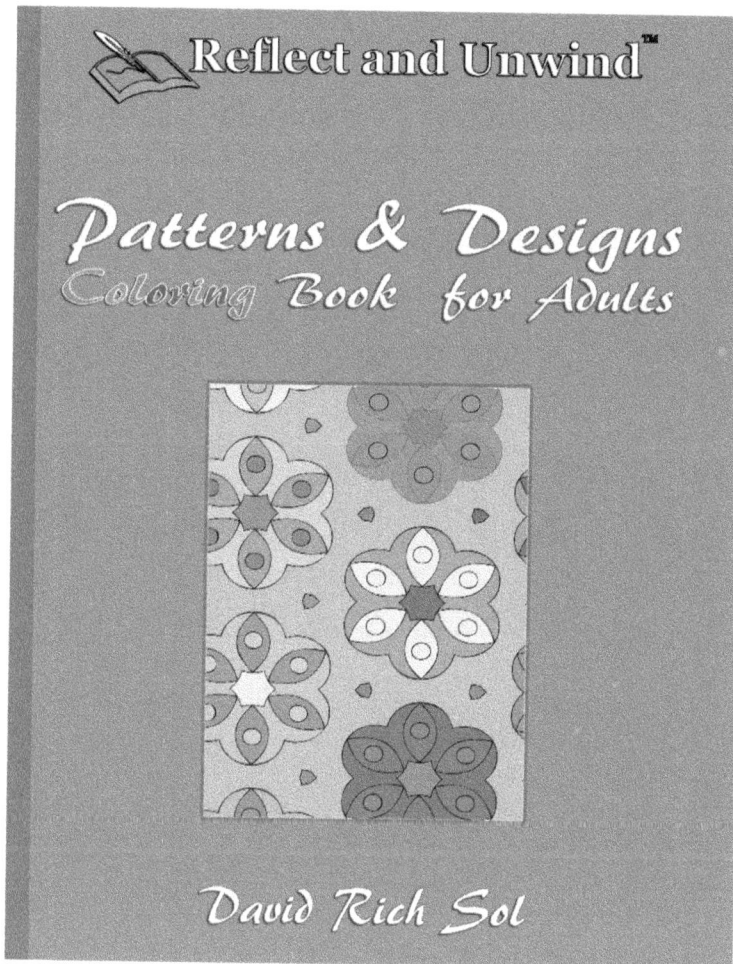

Enjoy 30, beautiful and detailed full-page patterns and designs as you relax, reflect and unwind. Get in touch with your inner artist—today!

To learn more about this book and all of our other current offerings, visit us online at http://www.ReflectandUnwind.com.

www.ingramcontent.com/pod-product-compliance
Lightning Source LLC
Chambersburg PA
CBHW080529030426
42337CB00023B/4680